# CHALLENGE

## Gyles Brandreth

### Illustrated by Peter Stevenson

A CAROUSEL BOOK

TRANSWORLD PUBLISHERS LTD.

# CHALLENGE

A CAROUSEL BOOK   0  552  54194  X

First published in Great Britain by Carousel Books

PRINTING HISTORY
Carousel edition published 1981

Text copyright © Gyles Brandreth 1981
Illustrations copyright © Transworld Publishers Ltd.
1981

Carousel Books are published by
Transworld Publishers Ltd.,
Century House, 61–63 Uxbridge Road,
Ealing, London W5 5SA.

Made and printed in United States of America
by Offset Paperbacks, Dallas, Pennsylvania.

# INTRODUCTION....

Are you the sort of person who likes a challenge?

If someone says to you: **'I bet you can't balance a book on your head and walk across the room,'** or **'I'm sure you couldn't pat your head with your left hand and rub your tummy with your right hand at the same time,'** do you automatically rise to the challenge?

**Can *you* balance a penny on each of your fingers, or an orange on your forehead? Are *you* able to whistle the National Anthem, or say the alphabet backwards?**

Very few of us can resist a challenge. It's probably because we don't like to be beaten, or have our friends do something we can't do. Not only that; it makes us feel good when we succeed.

In this book you will find hundreds of challenges for you to undertake. Not only challenges to do at home, but challenges for when you are on holiday or on a long and boring train journey or in the car. You can even take the book to school and challenge your friends—and your teachers.

You are sure to find this book of challenges a real challenge. I bet you won't be able to do them all!

# ORANGE JUICE

For this challenging
challenge you will
need **three oranges**.

Taking the first orange,
see if you can balance it
on your forehead—
you'll need to tip your
head back so that you
are facing the ceiling
to do this. See if you
can keep it there for
one minute.

When you have
perfected this test, try
balancing two oranges
on your head at
the same time.

In Birmingham there is an eleven-year-old boy who
can balance three oranges on his head for 92
minutes; that is a world record! You may not be able
to balance them on your head for that long, but
count how many seconds you can balance three
oranges on your head before they roll off. Take care
not to get orange juice on the carpet!

# PICK IT UP

**Can you:**

1. Lift a spoon—with one finger
   in the bowl and the
   thumb at the end?

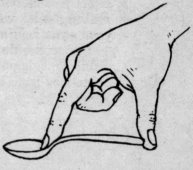

2. Lift four cotton reels
   between your thumb
   and first finger?

3. Pick up a marble with a fork and
   carry it across the room?

**4.** Lie on your back, pick up a cushion with your feet and raise it over your head, then drop it on the floor behind you?

**5.** Place a stick behind your knees, (a walking-stick would be ideal) bring your arms behind it and place your hands on the floor in front of you? While in this position pick up a matchbox from the floor with your teeth!

# BRAINBUSTERS: 1

Here are some challenges to get
the little grey cells in your head
working to full capacity!

**a.** Drawn here is an ordinary envelope.
All you have to do is copy the
illustration exactly, **BUT** you must do
so without once taking your pencil off
the page and without going over the
same line twice.

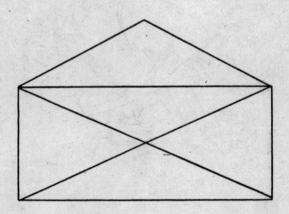

**b.** Emma missed her birthday last year.
It wasn't that she forgot it, and she
wasn't born on February the twenty-
ninth either, so how did she miss her
birthday?

**c.** An old man is 87½ years of age. His sister is 50. How many years ago was the old man 2.25 times as old as his sister?

**d.** A woman pointing to a portrait of a man said to her father, "That man's mother was my mother's mother-in-law." What relation was the woman to the subject of the portrait?

**e.** Which is heavier: a pound of feathers or a pound of gold?

**Answers on page 149.**

# PHYSICAL FEATS

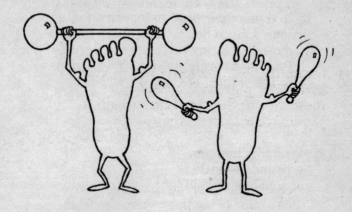

The following physical feats will really test your fitness and strength.

1. Clasp your hands together in front of your body, forming a loop, and jump through them with both feet.

2. Stand facing a wall and place the big toe of your left foot so that it touches the wall, about 30cm from the ground. Keeping your toe in this spot, hop over your left leg with your right without taking your toe from the wall.

3. Stand with your back against a wall, making sure that both your heels and the backs of your legs are touching the wall. Keeping your legs firmly against the wall, lean forward and try to touch your toes.

4. Lie on the floor, perfectly flat on your back. Fold your arms across your chest. Now try to stand up straight *keeping* your arms in that position.

5. Lie on the floor, again on your back. Lay your arms flat out on the floor beside you, palms downwards. Now lift your legs into the air and try to touch the floor above your shoulders, keeping your back and arms firmly on the floor. When you have done this, allow your legs to come back very very slowly and, just before your feet touch the floor again, hold them about eight centimetres from the ground for a count of ten. If you do this properly you will feel a slight pull in your tummy muscles.

# WORD PICTURES

D😊G

Here is a challenge that you can have great fun with—but it will need a little imagination, because to rise to the challenge you have got to **draw** words! It sounds crazy, but it can be done. Here are some examples of the word pictures to give you the idea:

L♡VE

SUNSET

🌳REE

NWOD ƎDISQU

SIDEWAYS

KICK

C☕P

TⅠE

FL◯AT

SINK

**Now the challenge is to write a short story using as many word pictures as you can.** You'll find it easy once you start. To date, the record for the most word pictures in one story is fifty—see if you can beat it.

Here is an example of a word picture story:

A LONG TIME AGO ON A BIG HILL A LITTLE FAT BOY LOOKED DOWN TOWARDS A TALL CHIMNEY IN THE DISTANCE.

If you cannot think of a story of your own, perhaps you would like to finish this one.

# HOW MANY?

**How well do you know your own house?** You probably think that you know it very well indeed, but if someone asked you how many windows it had, would you know? Do you know how many tiles are on the bathroom wall? How many lightbulbs there are to light the rooms when it is dark?

If you're not sure, then this is a very useful challenge. Take a piece of paper and find out the information below. When people write down information like this it is called an 'inventory', and often they list what is inside the house, just in case anything ever goes missing.

| ITEM | HOW MANY |
|------|----------|
| CHAIRS | |
| TABLES | |
| BEDS | |
| WINDOWS | |
| DOORS | |
| TELEPHONES | |
| LIGHTS | |
| MIRRORS | |
| CUPBOARDS | |
| RADIATORS | |
| TELEVISIONS | |
| RADIOS | |
| CLOCKS | |

**Now make a personal inventory of all the things that you have got and about yourself.**

Keep these inventories in a very safe and secret place, and the next time anyone asks you a question about yourself or your house—you will be able to give them the answer.

| YOUR NAME | HOW MANY |
|---|---|
| BOOKS | |
| TOYS | |
| BOARD GAMES | |
| RECORDS | |
| PENS AND PENCILS | |
| SOCKS | |
| SHOES | |
| PETS | |
| COATS | |
| PILLOWS ON YOUR BED | |
| DIFFERENT COLOURS IN YOUR BEDROOM | |
| PEOPLE IN YOUR FAMILY | |
| CHILDREN IN YOUR CLASS | |
| FRIENDS IN YOUR STREET OR ROAD | |

Don't forget to keep your inventory up-to-date.

# A-PEELING!

Here's a challenge you can try the next time you peel an apple—although do be extremely careful with the knife and make sure that it is not too sharp. If you are not allowed to peel your own apple, then challenge whoever peels the apple for you to do this.

The challenge is to take the peel off the apple in **one piece** so that you end up with one long spiral of peel. Some very clever adults are able to cut the peel very thinly and carefully so that they end up with a really long strip. The longest known peel stretched to 98 cm!

# THE MAN FROM ST. IVES

Without using a pencil and paper, a pocket calculator, or your fingers (let alone your toes), how quickly can you work out in your head the solution to this very old rhyme?

> As I was going to St. Ives,
> I met a man with seven wives,
> Each wife had seven cats,
> Each cat had seven kits.
> How many were going to St. Ives?

If you didn't know, there are actually two places called 'St. Ives' in Britain. The most famous is the picturesque town in Cornwall, the other is in Cambridgeshire near a place called Huntingdon. The latter has a famous statue of Oliver Cromwell in the market square. It will not, however, make any difference to the puzzle **which** St. Ives the man was going to!

**Answer on page 150.**

# FAMILY TREE

Have you ever thought how many people there are in your family and how they are all related? Not just your parents and brothers and sisters, but your grandparents, and aunts and uncles, your nephews and nieces and all your cousins. Find out how many people are in your family; ask your mother and father, and your grandparents, they will tell you who there is. **The challenge is to draw a family tree with everybody on it.** Start with yourself and work backwards.

Here is how your family tree might look:

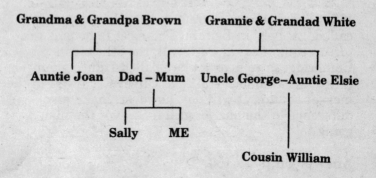

Some people are so interested in family trees that they study them all the time and they trace people's families back for hundreds of years. People who do this are called **'genealogists'**, and sometimes they discover that a family was related to or 'descended' from a famous King or Lord. Who would you like to be related to in history?

# PENNY PROBLEM

Take **ten 1p** coins, or ten ½p coins if you are not rich enough to have ten 1p's. Lay your left-hand palm downwards on the table and place one coin on each finger and balance it there.

You will find it easier if you balance the coin between your finger nail and the knuckle:

When you have the five coins balanced on your left hand, the problem is to get the other five coins on to your right hand, **without** any of the coins falling off.

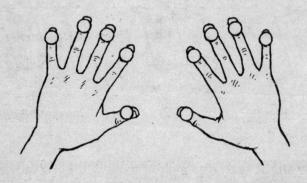

**Hint:** Lay the five coins for your right hand in a row along the edge of the table. Without having to move the fingers of your left hand too much, you can slide the coins off the table onto one finger at a time.

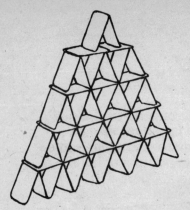

# HOUSE OF CARDS

This challenge will not only test your patience, it will also show you how steady your hands are.

All you need is a **pack of cards** and a surface that is not too slippery. **All you have to do is prop the cards up against each other to make a pyramid, like this:**

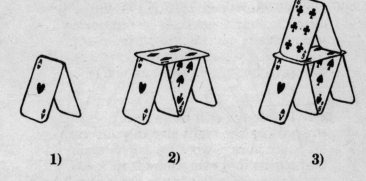

1)          2)          3)

One slight breeze or gust of wind will blow your card house across the room, so make sure there are no draughts before you start. The biggest card house ever built was made of twenty-two whole packs of cards (that is over 1100 cards!) but until you have become really expert, see if you can build a card house with just one pack of 52 cards.

# MAP IT OUT

People have been using maps for hundreds and
hundreds of years, not only to show them where to
go, but to show them the exact position of buildings
and roads in relation to the area. There will
certainly be a map printed of your area showing all
the roads in your town or city or part of the country;
it will even have marked on it rivers, churches,
railway lines, woodland areas, and bridges.
However, it may not feature your house in
particular, or the pillar box in front of your house, or
the three trees in your back garden.

**See if you can draw a very detailed
map of your area**, marking all the
houses, giving them their correct names
and numbers, marking in all the roads,
trees, shops, waste-paper bins, garages,
walls and fences, pillar boxes, and so on.

**The challenge will be to get
everything the right size in your map.**
Maps are always what we call 'to scale';
that means that everything is in
proportion, the pillar box is not bigger
than a house, and the pavement is not
bigger than the road.

Having drawn your map with all the
houses on it **see if you can write down
the name of every person that lives in
each of those houses.**

# SEASIDE TREASURE HUNT

The next time you are at the seaside have your very
own treasure hunt. This can be a challenge to do on
your own, but if you do it with friends you can see
who can collect **all** the treasure first.

**Here are the items you've got to collect:—**

1. **At least** six pebbles that
   resemble birds' eggs.
   Make sure they are **not**
   birds' eggs though!

2. One pretty coloured pebble. You will
   find many varieties of rocks and
   pebbles on most beaches, some will be
   streaked like marble, others will be
   blues and reds, even green. Choose
   one that you think is the prettiest of
   all.

3. **At least** three pure
   white feathers. Make
   sure that the bird has
   finished with them
   first!

**4.** Six or more *different* varieties of sea-shell.

**5.** A piece of sea-weed.

**6.** The largest sea-shell you can find.

If you do this with friends, set a time-limit for the hunt. The winner is the first person to collect the **minimum** number of **all** the items in the **least time**—BUT if someone else collects **more** 'bird's egg' stones, shells or feathers in the **full time-limit** then he will be the winner, not the person in first. Any ties can be decided by who has collected the largest sea-shell or the prettiest coloured pebble.

If you do this challenge on your own, you can set yourself a time-limit in which to complete the hunt—and see if you can beat your record on another day.

# TOWN TREASURE HUNT

If you live in a large town or city and won't be going
to the seaside for ages, you can have a treasure hunt
with your friends at home. As with the seaside
treasure hunt the challenge is to collect all the
treasure in the shortest possible time.

### Here is what you should collect:—

1. A **used** postage stamp.

2. A piece of silver-foil.
   A milk-bottle top
   will do.

3. A bus ticket.

4. A shiny 1p piece.

5. A ring-pull from a drinks can.

**6.** A piece of string 50cm long.

**7.** A leaf.

**8.** A drinking-straw.

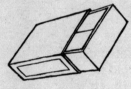

**9.** An empty matchbox.

**10.** An elastic band.

If you are feeling very generous and you invite your friends to join you in this challenge, perhaps you could give the winner a prize, providing of course that he or she can answer the following riddle:—

**What is it that the person who makes it does not need, the person who buys it does not use, and the person who uses it does so without knowing it?**

Do you know the answer? *A coffin.*

# BRAINBUSTERS: 2

More mental challenges to
test your brainpower!

**a.** Punctuate this sentence:

Brown where Briggs had had had had
had had had had had had had the
examiners' approval.

**b.** Pamela is twice as old as Peter used
to be when Pamela was as old as
Peter is now. Peter is now 18. How
old is Pamela?

**c.** In a library there are no two books
that contain the same number of
words. The number of books in the
library is greater than the number of
words in the largest book in the
library. How many words does the
book contain, and what is the book
about?

**d.** A hexagonal room had a cat in each
corner, five cats before each cat and a
cat on every cat's tail. How many cats
were there in this room?

**e.** Here is an island that has a very large moat around it. It is very deep and impossible to jump across. A man has to get on to the island urgently, but only has two planks exactly as long as the moat is wide so he cannot place the planks across the moat.

How can he get to the island without getting wet?

**Solutions on page 150.**

# COIN COLUMN

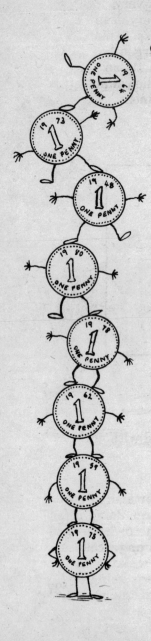

On January 30th, 1979, Richard Briers, actor and television star, knocked over the world's most valuable column of coins. The pile contained 27,530 ten pence pieces, which, if you are a mathematician you will know came to a total of £2753, which all went to a charity for handicapped children.

You may not have so many ten pence pieces, but you might have quite a number of **1p** pieces, so, as a challenge, **build a column of coins as high as you can.**

The very tallest column of pennies was one 11 feet 10 inches (4.26m) high that contained some 99,600 old pennies, which amounted to £415. This column of coins was knocked down on February 27th, 1970.

Do you think you could beat the record?

# CAN YOU DO THE CAN-CAN?

For this challenge you will need **two tin cans** and some **strong twine or string**. The cans will need to be really strong and quite large: big soup tins will do, but two empty paint tins (1 litre or 1.5 litre sizes) would be best.

Punch a hole into each side of the tin and thread your string through the holes making sure it is knotted securely. You will now have 2 stilts:—

**Taking extra special care not to fall off and hurt yourself, walk 20 metres on your tin can stilts.**

See if you **can**!

People have been walking on stilts for many hundreds of years, and not just children doing it for fun. In the south of France the shepherds have used them when tending to their sheep, simply because the ground is often under water and walking on stilts keeps their feet dry. What's more, being high off the ground they can see for long distances too.

# TAKE THE NUMBER

Travelling on long car journeys can often be very
boring and tiresome, even if you have friends with
you. But the time can soon pass very quickly if
you're faced with the right kind of challenge. The
next few challenges can all be done on a journey
whether it is by car or coach.

You can set yourself many challenges
with **car numbers**. Even when the roads
are not very busy you can still challenge
yourself by **trying to guess one letter
and one index number that will be on
the number plate of the next
approaching car.** For example, say to
yourself: there will be the letter **M** and
the number **3** on the next car, then if the
next car to come along has the
registration **PMC 435T** you will be right,
but if it is **JNV 897S** you will be wrong!

Another challenge is **to concentrate on
the lettering, and immediately you see
the three letters you must say the
first three worded sentence you can
think of,** even if it doesn't make sense.
For example, if you see the registration
JMC you might shout 'Jane Makes
Cakes', ELM might be 'Emma Loves
Mel', PLD 'Pigs Lie Down' and so on.
The object is to shout out the sentence as
soon as you see the letters.

## SPOTTING A CAR

If you are with friends, **look for letters that can spell words**. Two registrations MON and KEY will spell MONKEY, so look for the letters and spell the longest words you can.

On a busier road, **try to collect registration numbers in numerical order**. Look for a car that has just number **1** as its registration, and then look for them in order until you reach **100**. Or if you think this is too hard (and it is!) find a car with the registration number **111**, then look for **112**, then **113** and so on. Cars are registered from **1** to **999**, so on a long journey you will see thousands of cars, or you might like to do the challenge over a period of months, so that if on the last journey you reached **144**, you continue from that number. You **must**, however, collect them in order: if you see **125** and you are on **123**, it is no good if you have not spotted **124**.

**Another challenge is to each take the number of a car in turn, and add them up to a total of 1,000.** For example, John, Peter and Mary are in a car. Mary sees a car numbered 365, John 109, and Peter, 278. The next car to come along is 185 which makes Mary's total 550, John sees 476 making his total 585, and Peter sees 420 making his total 698. They carry on like this to see if they can reach exactly 1,000 BUT they must not go over 1,000. That is a challenge!

Alternatively you can perform the challenge in a different way **by taking the letters in turn.** Choose a word, for example the word CHALLENGE, then each take it in turn to look at the next car number. The first car may have the letters YCP so Mary writes down C, the next car may have HJV so John cannot write anything, and the next GHT meaning Peter cannot write anything. If Mary is lucky the next car will have an H in the registration so that she can write CH. The winner is the one who can write the word CHALLENGE first.

# WHAT A SPOT

There are many other challenges that can be undertaken on a journey that do not involve car numbers. You may be travelling in an area where there are few other vehicles, in which case searching for registration plates might be more tiresome than the journey! Do not despair, there are plenty more Brandreth challenges in store for you...

1. **Spot the clock.** As you go on your way through a town or city, count all the clocks you can see—not just public clocks and church clocks, but remember that many shops (especially jewellers) have clocks outside. Count 20 on a long journey.

2. **Spot the bridge.** On motorways, dual-carriage ways, and major roads, count the number of bridges you pass under and over.

3. **Spot the dog.** In this country we have many different breeds of dog. See exactly how many different breeds you can spot on one journey, and how many of each breed. The challenge will be to find which is the most popular dog in the country. Here is a list of the most common dogs you will see—tick them each time you see a particular dog. The number of ticks will tell you how many of each dog you have spotted.

**AFGHAN HOUND**
**AIREDALE TERRIER**
**ALSATIAN**
**AUSTRALIAN TERRIER**

**BASSET HOUND**
**BEAGLE**
**BEARDED COLLIE**
**BEDLINGTON TERRIER**
**BELGIAN SHEPHERD DOG**
**BERNESE MOUNTAIN DOG**
**BLOODHOUND**

**BOXER**

**BORDER COLLIE**
**BORDER TERRIER**

**BULLDOG**

**BULLMASTIFF**
**BULL TERRIER**

**CAIRN TERRIER**
**CHIHUAHUA**
**COLLIE**
**CORGI**
**CROSSBREED DOGS**
  **(MONGRELS)**

**DACHSUND**
**DALMATION**
**DOBERMANN**

**FOXHOUND**
**FOX TERRIER**

**CAVALIER**
**KING CHARLES**
  **SPANIEL**

**GREAT DANE**
**GREYHOUND**

**IRISH WOLFHOUND**
**JACK RUSSELL TERRIER**
**KING CHARLES SPANIEL**
**OLD ENGLISH SHEEPDOG**

**POODLE**
**PUG**
**PYRENEAN MOUNTAIN**
  **DOG**

**POINTER**

**RETRIEVER**

**SCHNAUZER**
**SEALYHAM TERRIER**
**SETTER**
**SPANIEL**—Cocker, Springer
**ST BERNARD**

**SCOTTISH TERRIER**

**WELSH CORGI**
**WEST HIGHLAND WHITE TERRIER**

**YORKSHIRE TERRIER**

4. **Spot the hats.** When riding along look out for pedestrians wearing hats—any kind of hat will do, a straw hat, a trilby, a bowler hat, an ornate feathered hat, and so on. Count 50 people wearing hats. Headscarves can be included and counted as hats as well.

**5. Spot the roadsign.** As you travel along you will see many different and varied road signs. Illustrated here are some of the road signs that you will see in this country. Spot at least one of each on your journey.

**6. Spot the statue.** Most towns and
cities have a statue somewhere to
commemorate a famous person who
was born there, or an event that
occurred in history. Count all the
monuments that you pass. Many
towns have a statue of Queen
Victoria, and usually a cenotaph or
war memorial. If you are passing
through London or any other major
city you should have no problems.

Count twenty on a journey through
built-up areas, ten if you are
travelling mainly through
countryside.

7. **Spot the policeman.** Years ago many policemen used to be 'on the beat'; they walked everywhere or travelled on a bicycle and each village had its local 'Bobby'—named after Sir Robert Peel. Today you find that policemen travel in police cars.

Count how many policemen and policewomen you see **on foot**. You can count policemen who are directing the traffic, but not any that you see inside a car or van.

A POLICEMAN
ON FOOT

A POLICEMAN
ON FEET

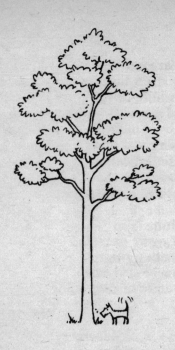

**8. Spot the tree.**
If you happen to be
driving through the
countryside, spot
at least 10 different
varieties of tree—
naming them all
correctly, of course.

**9. Spot the animal.** On your journey,
whether in a car, coach or train, look
out for animals along the roadside, in
the fields and in farmyards. You
might be surprised at how many you
see, and not only dogs and cats, but
horses and cows and goats and pigs
and sheep as well.

Count at least
six different
varieties of
animal.

A SPOTTED
DOG

**10.** If you are travelling with a group of friends, set yourselves the following challenge. **You must collectively spot these items:—**

Twelve street lamps.
Six sets of traffic lights.
Two roundabouts (not the fair-ground kind!)
One hospital.
One police-station.
Two multi-storey car parks.
Two supermarkets.
Two garages/petrol stations.
Six different breeds of dog.
Four churches.
A gasworks.
A woman with four children, including one in a pram.
A man wearing a hat.
A house with flowers in the garden.
Four red cars.
Four blue cars.
Four yellow cars.
One large lorry.

# EEEEEASY CHALLENGE

From a piece of paper cut out a very large letter 'E'. Then cut this letter into eight pieces like this:

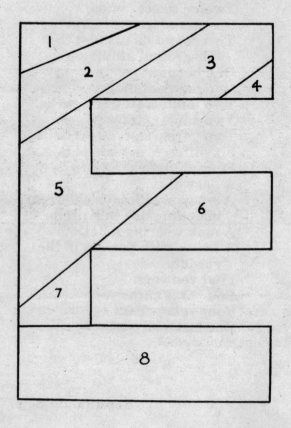

**Jumble up the pieces and, as a challenge, give the pieces to a friend and ask him or her to put them back together again.** Tell your friend that the pieces will form a letter of the alphabet but do not tell them **which** letter it will be.

# SHAPE THE FLOOR

Here is a piece of lino that's got to go onto the floor of a room that is perfectly square.

How would you cut the piece of lino so that it made a perfect square and the pattern matched perfectly as in the original piece?

**Solution on page 151.**

# WILL POWER

Having great will power is being able to resist the temptation of doing something you really want to do! If you've got will-power and can resist temptations, however great they may be, you're very, very lucky.

One challenge to test your will-power is to take something that you really enjoy, perhaps a bar of chocolate, and leave it lying in your room and keep yourself from eating it for at least **one week**. Buy it one week-end and say to yourself:

**'I will eat it *next* Saturday.'**

If you are to succeed in this challenge you will keep to your word, and you will enjoy the chocolate so much more when you do actually come to eat it!

Alternatively you can test your will-power when you are next faced with a cream cake or something equally delicious.

Sit and look at your tasty food and stop yourself from eating it for **ten minutes**.

There will certainly
be mouth watering
moments when
you crave to
take a bite...
but you must not.

That's will power!

45

# SILENCE IS GOLDEN

They do say that silence is golden, but have you ever **heard** silence? If you've ever gone to a very, very quiet place and sat very, very still and listened very, very carefully, you will know that there is rarely complete silence: there will be a noise of traffic in the distance, the buzz of an insect, the rustling of leaves, the singing of birds, the roar of an aeroplane overhead, or even just the sound of your heart beat.

It is possible, however, for YOU to remain silent— even though it is a great challenge to do so! Set aside a time for this challenge—for example, one complete morning—and keep silent throughout the period. **Whatever happens you must not utter a single word or make any noise of any kind.**

It's not nearly as easy as it sounds...

# ELBOW

All you need for this challenge is **a pile of coins**, say half a dozen two-pence pieces, and **an elbow**!

Simply position your elbow so that it's pointing out in front of you and place the pile of coins on top of it. Bring your hand down very quickly and catch the pile of coins before they reach the ground.

If you find it is too difficult then attempt the challenge with fewer coins or cheat and use a matchbox instead.

# BOUNCE, BOUNCE, BOUNCE.

**Take one bouncy football.**

1. Place your left hand behind your back and bounce the ball 50 times without stopping.

2. Repeat using your left hand.

3. Bounce the ball alternately between your left and right hands. Pat it with your right hand then with your left, and so on.

4. With your left hand behind your back, throw the ball into the air and by hitting it with your right hand keep it in the air for three minutes without once letting it drop on the ground.

5. Throw the ball between your right and left hand, keeping them at least 60 centimetres apart, and keep on for as long as you can without dropping it.

6. Throw the ball as high as you can into the air, making it go up in a straight line, and catch it when it comes down.

7. Throw the ball high into the air so that it curves in front of you, run forward and catch it before it hits the ground.

48

# DRINK IT

For this challenge, wear old clothes and perform it outside where it will not matter if some water spills on the ground.

Take a plastic cup of water and drink from the edge **furthest away from you** without spilling any!

# CROSS COINS

Take **seven coins** and lay
them out in a cross so
that there are **five vertically**
and **three horizontally**.

Lifting just two coins,
replace them so
that the horizontal line
and the vertical line
both have the same
number of coins
in them.

**Solution on page 151.**

# BRAINBUSTERS: 3

Here are some more amazing
mental challenges:

1. When the day after tomorrow is
   yesterday, today will be as far from
   Sunday as today was from Sunday
   when the day before yesterday was
   tomorrow. What day is it now?

2. If a man was born in 50 BC, how old
   was he on his birthday in 50 AD?

3. Lady Battersby pointed to a portrait
   on her wall saying: "I've no sister or
   brother, you may think me wild; but
   that man's mother was my mother's
   child." What relation was Lady
   Battersby to the man in the picture.

4. If I set my alarm clock to wake me up
   at 10 AM and I go to bed at 8 PM,
   how long do I sleep?

5. Write the number 10,000
   in a circle without
   lifting your pencil off
   the paper.

**Solutions on page 151.**

# GO BUST

If you have ever been to a museum or a stately home or a castle you will probably have seen a bust of a famous person. A bust is a statue, often lifesize, of a person's head and shoulders and it is usually made of marble or stone or plaster.

**Your challenge is to make a bust of one of your family or someone that you know.** It's quite easy once you know what to do, and if you are very careful you will end up with a beautiful statue that you can keep for years—and display in your museum or stately home or castle one day.

Here is what you need:—

> **As many old newspapers as you can find.**
> **A packet of wall-paper paste.**
> **Some water.**
> **An old washing-up bowl.**

Tear up some of the newspapers into very tiny shreds, about two centimetres square, and put them into your bowl. Mix together your wallpaper paste as the directions will tell you on the packet, and pour it into the bowl with your newspaper and leave it for a while so that it soaks into the newspaper.

After a time, if you give it a good stir, you will find that you are left with a grey doughy mass: this is known as **papier maché**. If it seems too dry add a little more paste; if it seems too runny add some more shredded newspaper.

It will help if you have a board to work on. Take a lump of the mixture and place it on to your board.

You will find that you can squeeze it and push it into any shape you like.

Keep some strips of dry newspaper close by. With the papier maché you will be able to mould the clay into a head. Form it into a ball to form the base of the head and push it in where the mouth would be, and where the eyes are.

Take small amounts of the papier maché and give your sculpture a nose, ears, lips, eyes, cheek bones, hair, and so on.

Once you have achieved the desired shape, lightly press some of the dry newspaper pieces onto your sculpture. You will find that they will stick on quite easily because they soak up the paste.

When you have finished your sculpture, leave it in a warm place to dry out. Because it is solid papier maché it may take several days, but when it does dry completely you will find it is rock hard and even if you drop it it will not break. When it is dry you can paint it as you wish. If you paint it with some white glossy paint it will look exactly like the marble busts you see in castles and palaces, but you may prefer to make it life-like by painting it flesh coloured. If you want it to look really authentic you can stick on crepe hair or wool.

You don't have to make your bust out of solid papier maché. You can give yourself a head start (!) by using a different 'base'. Simply roll dry newspaper sheets into a ball and put them inside a paper bag so that the newspaper fills the bag out completely and is quite solid. Use this as a base and add your papier maché on top of it to make your head. It has also been known for people to cheat! As their base, the cheats use a cheap polystyrene wig head, available in many large department stores, cover it with papier maché and paint it. Half the hard work has already been done for them.

Once you become really expert at handling papier maché you will find that you can create exciting masks with it as well. In fact almost anything can be made out of papier maché and it is frequently used in the theatre to make props, from suits of armour to roast chickens.

As an extra challenge, try to create an item of food—a bun or a cake, a sausage or a pork chop, even a loaf of bread—and make it look as realistic as possible. If it looks really life-like put it in the fridge and see how long it takes for anyone to spot the fact that it's a fake.

# LAY A GOLDEN EGG

**I'm challenging you to create a golden egg.** No, you're not allowed to paint a real hen's egg gold. You've got to make the golden egg yourself.

If you have tackled the last challenge you will know all about papier maché. The principle of making a golden egg is very similar.

You need to begin with a balloon. Blow it up until it is roughly egg-shaped. Take a bowl of paste and some strips of newspaper. Dip the strips into the paste one at a time and stick them on to the balloon so that they overlap. Make sure that you have at least three layers of paper **all over** the balloon:—

When it is completely covered, give it a couple of days to dry really rock hard. Now comes the exciting bit. When it is really hard, take a pin, push it through the paper and burst the balloon inside! You will now be left with a hollow egg. All you have to do is paint it gold, and you have your very own giant golden egg—the perfect present for any goose you happen to know!

# FUNNY FACES

I am sure you would feel very insulted if people said
that you have a funny face (and I'm sure you
haven't!) but **I challenge you to make the funniest
face you can and see how long you can stay like
that**! It will help if you sit in front of a mirror, but,
whatever you do, you must not laugh!

First of all, push out your tongue
as far as it will go, and make sure
that it stays out all the time.
Then screw up your face to make
the most hilarious face you can.

Believe it or not, there are actually people who take
the art of pulling funny faces very seriously indeed
and call this 'skill' by the name of 'gurning'. So if
you practise this you could become a National
Gurning Champion.

# MUMS AND DADS

Pictured here are six cards with three different mums and dads on. So there are three mums and three dads. They are all placed in a row so that each mum is next to a dad. Can you in **three moves** make it so that all the mums are together and all the dads are together? No gaps must be left and each move you must move two neighbouring cards. You should end up with them as in figure **II**.

**I**

**II**

Solution on page 153.

# SPIN THE COIN

For this challenge you will need a coin with a **milled**
edge, which means you will need either a 5p piece or
a 10p piece as one and two pence pieces have a
smooth edge. A milled edge was originally put onto
coins several hundreds of years ago when people
used to 'clip' coins. In the days when coins were not
perfectly round people could clip off small pieces and
nobody would notice. They would then melt down all
the pieces they had collected and make themselves
another coin. The milled edge was introduced to put
a stop to this illegal practice.

Take your modern milled edge coin and
find two pins. Place the coin between the
two points of the pins and it will stay
there because of the milled edge. Hold it
in the air and blow very gently onto the
coin to make it spin. **See if you can
keep it spinning for at least sixty
seconds.**

# CATCH IT

Take an ordinary **sheet of writing paper.** Get a friend to stand on a chair and drop the piece of paper from a great height. **All you have to do is catch the piece of paper between your finger and thumb before it reaches the ground.** Easy? Don't you believe it!

Next get your friend to drop a **blown-up balloon** for you. You must catch it with **one** hand only.

Finally, get the person to drop down some **curtain rings** or small hoops, which you must catch on one finger!

# FISHY CHALLENGE

Here are four fishermen. You will see that one of them has managed to hook a very large fish, but unfortunately their lines have become so tangled up that they do not know which one it is. Can you unravel the lines and see which fisherman has caught the fish?

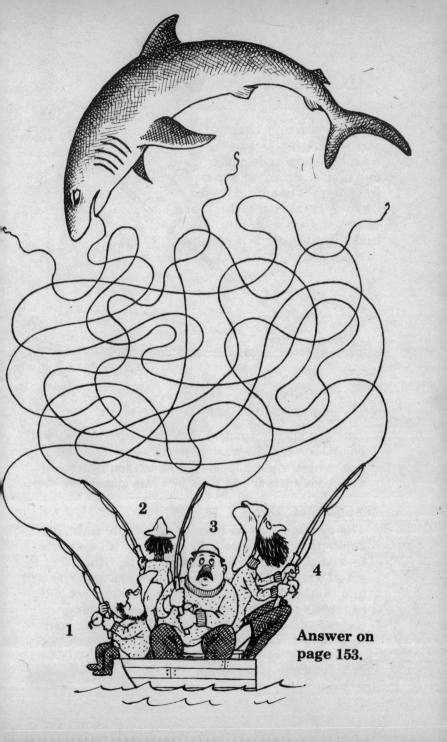

Answer on page 153.

# BIG FEET

This is a silly but not-so-easy challenge and should be undertaken the next time someone calls you 'Big feet' which could happen if you accidentally tread on somebody's toe or put your foot into something you shouldn't!

**The challenge is to take every single pair of socks that you have and put them all on your feet at the same time, one after the other.** Try to get at least ten pairs of socks on if you can. You will find that with each pair you put on, your feet will look bigger and eventually your feet will be so enormous that you won't even be able to get your shoes on!

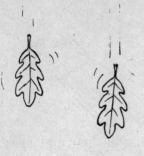

# AUTUMN LEAVES

When Summer draws to a close and Autumn approaches you will find that many trees start shedding their leaves all over the ground. First of all, however, they will turn beautiful shades of orange, yellow and gold. On a fine Autumn day, go out into the country and collect as many **different** fallen leaves as you can. You will find many different shapes and sizes as well as colours.

**Only pick up the leaves that are on the ground:** never pull them directly from the tree. The tree will drop them when it is ready! Pick up only leaves that are whole and are not too crunchy and flaky so that they will stay in one piece. Keep them all in a plastic bag until you arrive home.

When you get home, sort through all the leaves and lay them on to a piece of card. Looking at the shapes of the leaves, identify exactly which tree they came from. You can stick the leaves on to card if you wish and label them correctly, which will give you a permanent reminder of your expedition. If you are artistic, stick them down and make a collage picture from them. If you cover the card with sticky-backed plastic your picture will remain intact for many years to come.

# CRACK THE CODE

Spies and secret agents always send their messages in code. Can you decipher these ones?

1. TH ERAI NINS PAINF ALLSMAI
   NLYO NTH EPL AIN.

2. HIST SI UITEQ A HALLENGEC
   UTB OTN IFFICULTD ORF
   OMEONES HOW SI EALLYR
   LEVERC.

3. TEEM EM THGINOT TA EHT DLO
   HCRUHC TA THGINDIM.

4. EW EAR GBEIN DWATCHE YB NA
   YENEM TAGEN.

5. ANC OYU RCCKA SHTI EDCO TI SI
   YRVE TUIFIDFCL.

6. IFYO UWAN TTOK NOWTH ESEC
   RETPAS SWOR DITI SSAUS AGES.

7.  CQIHJ KMTHINKBD ADROBERTSD
    PJISWZ DFAGB JKCOUNTERLA
    PBSPYXS WCANDTG UYISPT
    NCWORKINGDI YFFORLW
    YGTHESO OGENEMYJU
    RXAGENTLM.


8.  Can you work out what this secret
    message says:

    Y Y U R Y Y U B I C U R Y Y 4 M E  ?

Solutions on page 153.

# TEAR OFF A STRIP

This is one of those seemingly simple challenges that isn't as easy as it looks.

Take a sheet of paper and make **two** cuts in it like this:—

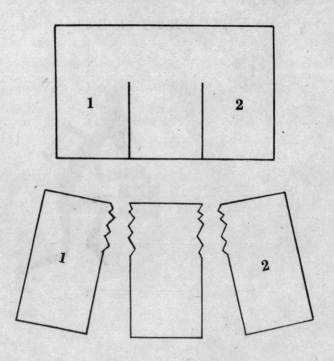

Hold the two outer pieces marked **1** and **2** and give them a sharp pull so that they both pull away from the centre piece and you are left with three pieces.

# JOIN THE DOTS

Illustrated here are twelve dots, arranged in 3 rows
of 4 dots in each row. You will see that the dots can
be joined in many ways by six straight lines, BUT
can you join the dots using only **five**?

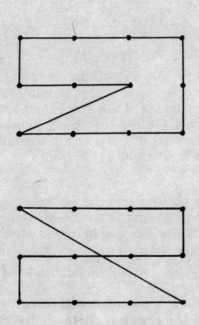

**Solution on page 154.**

# HOW FAR?

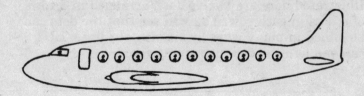

At Heathrow airport a small private plane is waiting
to take twenty-two passengers to Madrid. As the
passengers get on board the plane the hostess shows
each person to his or her seat. Some people prefer to
sit right at the back of the plane in the tail, while
others choose to sit right at the front.

The pilot is in position and the plane is ready for
take off. Each passenger is now in his or her seat.
They will, of course, be able to have a meal on the
plane to pass the time.

**Can you work out who will have
travelled the greatest distance by the
time the plane reaches Madrid?**

**Solution on page 154.**

# WORD SQUARE

Below is a word square. It's like a crossword puzzle without any clues.

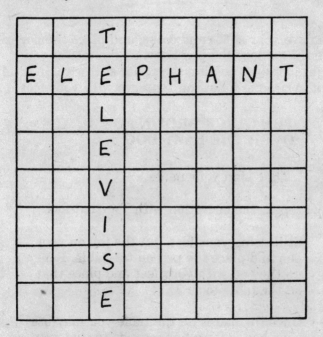

**The challenge is to fill in the square making as many real words going down and across as you can.**
Two words have already been put in to help (or hinder) you.

You are allowed to put in blanks. For every word you put in you score one point. For every blank you put in you lose half a point. Give the challenge to your friends and see if they score more than you.

# GET IT WRITE

Take a **large pad of paper** and a **felt-tipped pen.**

Remove your shoes and socks, and place the paper on the floor. Place the pen between the toes of your right foot and, holding the paper still with your left foot, write the following sentence with your foot:

**THE QUICK BROWN FOX JUMPS
OVER THE LAZY DOG**

Then sign your name.

Now repeat the operation with your left foot.

Still using your feet, put the top on your pen and place the pen on the table. Pick up the pad with your feet and place that on the table too.

Once the pad is on the table you may use your hands for a few seconds so that you can find a clean page on your pad, then remove the top from the pen and place the pen in your mouth. Hold the pad still and try writing the same sentence with the pen in your mouth.

You will find that with practice you will be able to write quite neatly with your mouth. The challenge is learning how to apply the pressure when you wish to write; you will find it **very** odd at first!

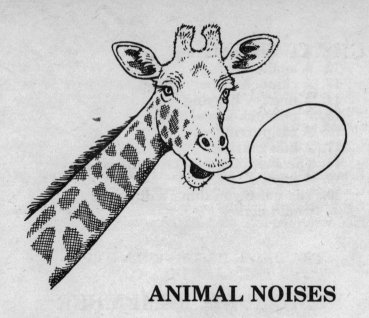

# ANIMAL NOISES

How clever are you at imitating animals? For
example, do you know what sound a giraffe makes?
Apart from the crunching of leaves it makes no other
noise at all! So that would not be too difficult to
imitate, but here are some more animals. Make a
noise as close as you can to resemble that of the
animal.

1. A puppy crying.
2. A dog barking.
3. A cat miaowing.
4. A cow mooing.
5. A sheep bleating.
6. A duck quacking.
7. A goose honking.
8. An elephant trumpeting.
9. A pig grunting.
10. A horse whinnying.

71

11. A mouse squeaking.
12. A snake hissing.
13. A rhinoceros bellowing.
14. A donkey braying.
15. A peacock screeching.
16. A cat purring.
17. A lion roaring.
18. The snapping of a crocodile's jaws.
19. A pigeon cooing.
20. The noise you think a dinosaur would make.

# REMEMBER, REMEMBER

How good is your memory? Can you remember dates or names or faces? If you think you have got a good memory, see just how long it takes you to learn this poem so that you know it off by heart and can recite it without even looking at the book.

## Grandma's Advice

*"Help yourself, help yourself, little boy—do:*
*Don't wait for others to wait upon you."*
*Grandma was holding her afternoon chat,*
*Knitting and rocking away as she sat.*
*"Look at the birds, how they build their own nest!*
*Watch the brown bees, always toiling their best!*
*Put your own hands to the plough, if you'd thrive,*
*Don't waste your moments in wishing, but strive."*
*Up in her face looked a mischievous elf:*
*"Don't forget darling," said she, "help yourself."*

*Afternoon shadows grew drowsy and deep:*
*Grandma was tranquilly folded in sleep.*
*Nothing was heard but the old farmhouse clock*
*Plodding away with its warning "tick, tock!"*
*Out from the pantry there came a loud crash:*
*Pussy jumped up from the hearth like a flash.*
*Back to her chair strode the practical boy.*
*Grinning, he cried, "Please, I've upset the shelf:*
*Grandma, I minded; I **did** help myself."*

When you know it by heart, recite it to your family,
especially Grandma!

# EVERYDAY NOISES

This is a much noisier and more difficult challenge. See how clever you are at making the following sounds—and if you are very good you might get yourself a job in the BBC sound effects department!

1. A grandfather clock ticking.
2. The dialling tone of a telephone.
3. A clock being wound up.
4. A door creaking.
5. A car starting.
6. A champagne bottle opening.
7. A glass smashing.
8. A baby crying.
9. A door slamming.
10. A train going very fast.
11. A steam train.
12. A car horn.
13. A bicycle bell.
14. A camera clicking.
15. Gas escaping.
16. A vacuum cleaner.
17. A church bell tolling.
18. Footsteps on a country road.
19. Horses hooves.
20. A gun being fired.

To create these sounds you must do them *all* vocally, using only your tongue, teeth, mouth, and vocal chords. You must have no other help.

# CHARITY CHALLENGE

In this country you will find that there are many
important and worthwhile charities that desperately
need money to help them with their good work.
There are charities to help people who are blind,
people who are seriously ill, people who are
handicapped, people who are old, charities to look
after animals and birds. Perhaps you have a
particular charity that you would like to help; maybe
you would like to help raise money to buy a guide-
dog for a blind person or help towards preserving
wildlife. You can find addresses for all your local
charities at your library.

Raising money for a charity is certainly a
challenge—and here are three ways you can help do
it.

1. **Hold your own garden fête.** Collect
   any old toys, articles of clothing,
   ornaments, games, and so on so that
   you can set up several little stalls. It
   would be a good idea to involve
   several grown-ups at this stage. Make
   some posters to advertise that you are
   having a fête, giving the date and
   time. Collect as many items to sell as
   you can. Your parents might make
   little buns and cakes, and provide
   some orange squash so that you can
   have a refreshments stall. Get all your
   friends to help, and make sure that as
   many people as possible come along.

75

Have one person at the gate collecting just a couple of pence from each person as an entrance fee. If you charge, say, 2p and twenty people come you've raised 40p before you've even started!

Don't just have stalls where people can buy things: have games and activities as well, charging them 1p a go.

For example, if your parents will let you (and do ask permission first), mark off a small piece of the garden for a treasure hunt and carefully bury a 10p piece where it cannot be seen. Collect lots of small sticks (sticks from ice lollies are ideal) and charge your guests 1p to take a lollie stick and write their name on it. They must then push it into the ground at the spot where they think the treasure is buried. At the end of the fête the person whose stick is nearest the buried 10p wins it!

Organise lots of different activities—from bowling skittles to pinning the tail on the donkey—and charge everyone 1p a turn.

'Guess the name of the doll' is always a popular challenge. Take an old doll and smarten it up, put new ribbons in the hair, make some new clothes so that it looks as nice as possible. Again for a penny, get people to guess its name. First, you must choose a name for it, such as Jemima or Emma or Sebastian or Frederick or Gyles. Write the name you choose on to a piece of paper and seal it in an envelope and tell **no-one**. When people come to guess the doll's name you have a long list and get them to write their name on the list and their guess. If you choose a very unusual name nobody will guess and you can keep the doll! But it would be nice if someone does guess it and you can present the doll to them. At the end of the afternoon, gather everyone around and get someone to open the envelope and read out the name.

You'll find a lot of money can be raised in a very short time. The challenging part is organising your fête and making sure it is a success. Good luck!

2. If you have only a very small garden and cannot hold a garden fête, there are still other challenges that will raise money. A popular one which you can do with your friends is **your very own sponsored walk**. First of all you will have to decide upon the charity you want to support. Then give each of your friends taking part a special sheet with their name on like this:

| On SATURDAY 14th APRIL at 2.00pm JEREMY BROWN will be taking part in a sponsored walk to raise money for the R.S.P.C.A. | |
|---|---|
| **SPONSOR** | **AMOUNT PER KILOMETRE** |
| | |
| | |
| | |
| | |
| | |

Each person taking part can then take this to all his friends and relations and if they are kind they will sponsor him or her and promise to give them so much per kilometre, perhaps a penny or even five pence.

You must decide too on the route you are all going to take and the distance it is going to be. It is important to get an adult to help you organise this, or if you belong to a youth club or the scouts or guides, you may like to suggest to the leader that you have a sponsored walk to help a charity and then they will organise it with you.

3. If you want a challenge on your own and cannot do a sponsored walk, sponsored cycle ride, or sponsored swim, you can always be a **sponsored helper around the house** and see if people will give you a few pennies to do the washing-up, or mow the lawn, or clean the car, or even 5p a week to keep your bedroom especially tidy! If you do this for a few weeks or a couple of months you will find the money will soon add up for you to send to the charity of your choice.

# BUBBLES!

Can you blow a bubble with Bubble Gum? If so you can tackle this challenge, which is to **blow the biggest bubble you can.** The greatest bubble gum bubble ever blown was 48.9 cms in diameter and was blown by 18 year old Susan Montgomery of California in 1979.

The biggest bubble blown in the United Kingdom was 41.91cms and this was achieved by 13 year old Nigel Fell from Northern Ireland, also in 1979.

If you practise very carefully you might be able to blow the biggest bubble in your neighbourhood, and possibly eventually you will be able to blow the biggest bubble in the world. **All you need to do is blow one 49 cms in diameter and you will be a record breaker!**

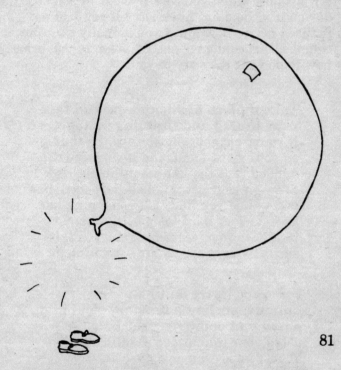

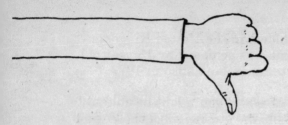

# THUMBS DOWN

Most of us tend to take our thumbs for granted; they are there on our hands, they are useful for sucking, for waving in the air to show your approval of something, they enable you to count up to ten on your hands, and you can place them against the tip of your nose when you cock-a-snook at somebody, but do you use them for much else? If you had not realised before how much you actually use your thumbs, this challenge should prove to you exactly how important they are to you.

**Take a piece of sticky tape and tape your thumb and first fingers together.** If you are right-handed tape the thumb on your right hand, and if you are left-handed tape the left-hand thumb. Now carry on as if nothing had happened, but every time you find that something has become very hard to do because of your lack of thumb, write it down. You'll be surprised how long your list will become.

For example, try **doing up your buttons, peeling a banana, picking up a ball and combing your hair**, without using your thumb. It's so difficult it's almost impossible!

82

# IT'S HANDY

If you rose to the last challenge you will realise how valuable your thumbs are. If you have ever broken an arm (and I do hope you never have!) you will also know that with an arm in a sling it is very difficult to carry on with your normal day to day life.

To find out how much you need your arm, when you get up one morning, **put your right arm** (If you are right-handed) **across your midriff, and button your shirt or blouse up over it** so that you cannot use it at all.

Now spend as much of the day as you can like this and see how difficult life is. It will make you appreciate your arms much more.

# THE EYES HAVE IT

Now that you have established exactly how important your limbs are to you, and how difficult life would be without them, see how you would cope without being able to see. You will find this a real challenge.

Begin by blindfolding yourself, or get somebody to blindfold you, and try to dress yourself and comb your hair. Before you start make sure that you know exactly what obstacles are in the room so that you will be able to guide yourself around them and not hurt yourself.

Now make your way to the table and **eat your breakfast** still blindfolded. Pour some cornflakes into a bowl and put the milk and sugar on yourself. Try to pour yourself a cup of tea. See how difficult it is to eat and drink when you cannot actually see what you are doing. See what it is like buttering toast in the dark and finding out where the marmalade jar is. At first you will need the help of your family to guide you.

Again this challenge to go about your business without being able to see will really make you appreciate your eyes. You will also realise how, when blindfolded, your powers of taste, smell, touch, and hearing become doubly important to you. This is a challenge that will make you aware of your whole body.

# A CUT ABOVE

Can you lift a knife? It sounds easy doesn't it? Well, yes it is, but can you lift **five** knives? That might be easy too, **except the challenge is to lay four of the knives down on the table and lift them all with the other knife, the fifth.**

Solution on page 154.

# NUMBER PICTURES

Here are two challenges for people who like numbers and pictures:—

**1.** Here are the numbers 1–9. Take a pencil and turn each of the numbers into a certain object. (For example, add ear pieces to number 8 and you'd have a pair of spectacles.)

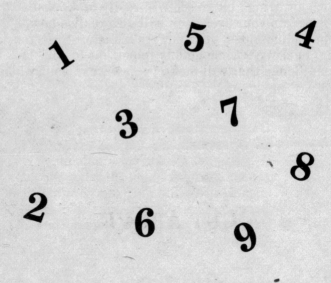

**2.** Take a blank sheet of paper and on it draw a face using only numbers and nothing else. (For example, a 7 could be the nose, the hair could be made up of hundreds of 3's and so on.)

# BRAINBUSTERS: 4

Here are some even more difficult mental challenges to help you improve your brain power.

    **a.** When is it legal for a man to marry his daughter?

**b.** Peter can run a kilometre in 4.12 minutes. Paul can run 4.12 kilometres in an hour. Which do you think is the fastest runner?

    **c.** Three cannibals and three missionaries have to cross a river. For obvious reasons the cannibals must never be allowed to outnumber the missionaries, and only one cannibal can row. The boat can only hold three passengers. How do they make the journey?

**d.** The age of Mr. Wood added to that of his daughter totals exactly 100 years. Mr. Wood's age multiplied by four and divided by nine gave a figure which was equal to his daughter's age. Can you work out what both their ages were?

**e.** Make up a short sentence using all the letters of the alphabet. If you're really clever you will know that one has already appeared in this book!

**f.** An artist was painting a portrait of himself—what's called a 'self-portrait'—and although he was a very good artist, the portrait did not really look quite like him. Can you think why this would be?

**g.** A six-sided figure is called a hexagon. What is a seven-sided figure called?

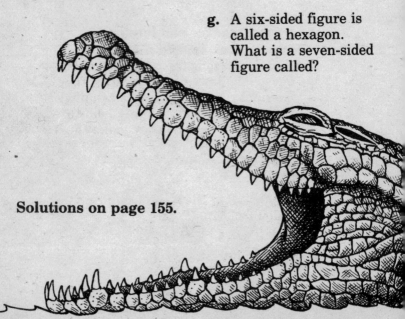

Solutions on page 155.

# HOW MANY?

Are you good at counting?

If so how many triangles are there in this figure? **Count them all.**

Try shading them in in different colours. It might help.

**Solution on page 156.**

# JOGGING ALONG

Running can be very good for you. It helps your breathing, it helps your muscles grow strong, it improves your general fitness and stamina. You may get a lot of exercise at school, playing sport, and in the playground, but do you sometimes get out of breath or feel that you would like to be able to run a little faster?

This challenge can be fun to do and will keep you fit and healthy at the same time. Begin one Monday morning by running on the spot for 30 seconds before you go on to school, and repeat it again in the evening when you get home. Lift your knees up as high as they will go and swing your arms at the same time.

The next morning run on the spot for 1 minute and again when you get home from school.

On Wednesday morning run for 1½ minutes, and so on, increasing it by 30 seconds every day until you reach 3½ minutes. Always attempt this challenge **before** breakfast; never immediately after a meal.

When you begin to feel really fit and can run on the spot for 3½ minutes without getting out of breath, you can start jogging properly. Begin by jogging around the garden in the morning, and then progress to jogging to school or jogging to the bus stop. Perseverance is the key word if you want to succeed with this challenge. It's no good lying in bed one morning because you feel too lazy to run. If you do you will not have risen to the challenge.

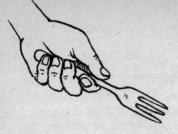

# FORK IT OUT

## Challenge I

Take a bowl of your favourite soup, minestrone, tomato, vegetable, chicken, whatever you really enjoy most, and eat it—with a FORK!

If you find it too much of a challenge, take a very small spoon, such as an egg spoon, and attempt to eat it as fast as you can with that, making sure you eat every drop of soup and you don't get indigestion.

As a third alternative you can drink your soup with a straw.

## Challenge II

Place 2 cream crackers or water biscuits in a dish and eat them with a knife and fork, not touching them with your fingers.

And if you're crackers about cream cracker challenges—challenge a friend to eat **and swallow** 3 cream crackers, without having a drink while doing so, before you can manage to drink half a pint (250 ml) of orange juice using a teaspoon! It's said that the orange juice drinker always wins this race—do you think that's true?

# TRICKY TRIANGLE

Here is a triangular pattern. Can you copy it on to a
piece of paper (or trace it) **without lifting your
pencil off the paper** once you have started,
**without going over the same line twice**, and
**without crossing over a line that you have
already drawn.**

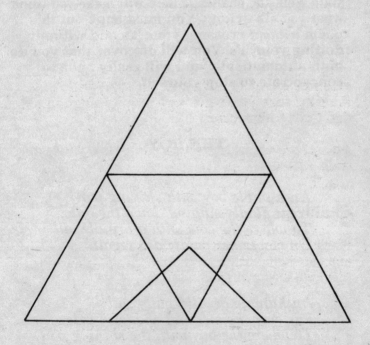

**Solution on page 156.**

# NO DOTS OR CROSSES

It often takes us a very long time to learn to do proper, neat, joined-up handwriting, but once we do master the technique it comes perfectly naturally to us for the rest of our lives and we write without even thinking about it. If, for example, you were going to write the word 'elephant' you would do so without thinking. You wouldn't say to yourself: 'Oh, that's an 'e' and an 'l' and another 'e'.....' and so on. Would you? Well, the challenge here will make you think what you are writing. **You must copy out this poem *without* crossing your 't's and without dotting your 'i's. You will discover that you do both automatically and will really have to concentrate to stop yourself.**

### THE BOY

*An humble boy with shining pail,*
*Went gladly singing down the dale,*
*To where the cow with a brindle tail*
*On clover her palate did regail.*


*An humble bee did gaily sail*
*Far over the soft and shadowy vale,*
*To where the boy with the shining pail,*
*Was milking the cow with the brindle tail.*

*The bee lit down on the cow's left ear,*
*Her heels flew up through the atmosphere—*
*And through the leaves of a chestnut tree,*
*The boy soared into futurity.*

Challenge a friend to a writing race and see
which of you can write out the poem first,
without crossing any t's and any i's.

# NEEDLE THROUGH A BALLOON

This is a cross between a challenge and a magic trick. Once you have mastered the challenge you can turn it into an illusion with which to amaze your friends.

**The challenge is to take an ordinary balloon, blow it up and push a knitting needle right through it so that it goes through one side and comes out of the other without the balloon bursting.**

You may think that it is impossible, but there is a way of doing it if you are careful.
Simply take two pieces of sellotape and stick one on each side of the balloon.
If you then push the needle through the places where the sticky tape is you should find that it will go straight through and the balloon will not burst.

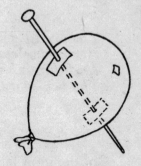

When you have completed the challenge you will be able to perform it in front of friends, but don't tell them about the sticky tape. You can even give them an ordinary balloon and a needle and see if they can do it. Of course, the balloon will burst every time they try it. Only you will know the secret!

# TOWER OF DRAUGHTS

This challenge will take a great deal of patience and ingenuity. All you need is a set of draughts with which you must build a tower as high as you can— not in a pile, **but like this**:

Begin by placing four draughts on their side to make a cross as shown in this aerial view. Then lay four flat on top of that, and build the tower up in this manner as high as you can. Be careful not to make a draught or your tower will collapse!

# ASSAULT COURSE

Get together with some friends and gather as many objects as you can to make an assault course in your garden!

Old cardboard boxes, rubber tyres, barrels, ropes, tea chests, and anything else that you can find which you can jump over, swing on, climb through, climb over, and so on.

When you have gathered all the items, set them out in a suitable part of your garden where they are not going to be in anybody's way, and make sure that everything is perfectly safe. If you have a wooden crate, for example, make sure there are no sharp nails sticking out of it.

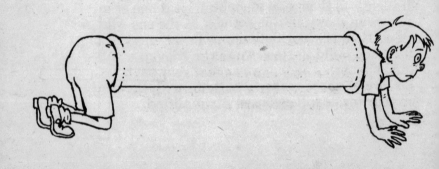

Set out the course so that each of your
friends knows exactly what to do. For
example, you might have to start by
crawling through a cardboard box,
jumping over a rope, climbing through a
tyre that is hanging from a tree,
clambering over a chair, squeezing
through a barrel, running twice around a
pile of twigs, and end up by jumping two
metres over two pieces of string that you
are pretending mark a deep river.

Once you have planned the course, each
of your friends must attempt it one at a
time. The champion will be the one who
can complete the course in the shortest
amount of time. **To make it even
harder you can suggest that each
person carries a balloon with them. If
it bursts, they are disqualified.**

# CAMERA CHALLENGE

If you or someone you know has a camera you can take a picture so that it appears that you have a very small person standing on your hand.

All you need to do is to take a picture of two people. One stands close to the camera with his or her hand out to one side. The second person stands a long way behind the first. If you line them up carefully in the eye of your camera you can make it appear that one is standing on the other's hand. The challenge will only succeed when the picture is developed and you can see it has worked!

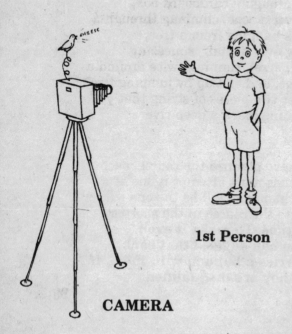 

**2nd person several metre behind**

**1st Person**

**CAMERA**

**You must aim to get a picture like this!**

# DAFT DEFINITIONS

FACSMILE

Here are some words that have been given a
definition, but unfortunately not all the definitions
are correct. **The challenge is to guess which
words have correct definitions and which don't.**
Once you have made up your mind, take an ordinary
English dictionary and look up each of the words in
turn to see which have been defined correctly.

1. **ABADDON**—Something that is not very good.
2. **ABOMINATE**—Dislike intensely
3. **ACQUIESCE**—To communicate with.
4. **BESMIRCH**—To discolour or sully.
5. **BOBBIN**—A ship for deep sea fishing.
6. **BY-WAY**—A secret passage.
7. **CACHE**—A hole in the ground.
8. **CANNOPY**—A small cannibal.
9. **CASCARA**—Make-up for eyelashes.
10. **CHIROPODIST**—Someone who looks at your
    hands.
11. **DEPICT**—To put down.
12. **DIRE**—Dreadful, terrible.
13. **DORY**—A clock.
14. **ELEMENTAL**—Mad as a hatter.
15. **ENOW**—Just now.
16. **EXCERPT**—To overstate.
17. **FACSMILE**—A big grin.
18. **FILBERT**—A nut.
19. **GLAIVE**—A sword.

20. **HANK**—Good looking.
21. **IGNOBLE**—Of humble or low birth.
22. **ILLUDE**—To escape from.
23. **LABORIOUS**—In a maze or labyrinth.
24. **LUCID**—Clear or transparent.
25. **MACABRE**—Beautiful.
26. **MULLOCK**—Rubbish or rubble.
27. **OHM**—A Cockney's house.
28. **POTHER**—A cloud of dust.
29. **SEVER**—To grow in soil.
30. **TRANTER**—A Pedlar.

# SNOWTIME

Here's a challenge for the deep mid-winter when the snow is thick on the ground.

Make sure that you wrap up warmly, with hat and scarf, boots, at least two pairs of socks, a thick sweater, a coat, and anything else you need to protect you from the cold, then go out wearing thick gloves and begin by making a snowball. Heap it together in your hands until it is solid and about the size of a football. Then lay it on the ground, but don't kick it! Instead roll it along the ground, and you'll find that as you do so it will pick up more snow and increase in size. Before very long it will be as big as you are and eventually it will get so heavy that you will be unable to push it.

When you reach this stage, you'll have the body of a snow-man. Make another snowball to give him a head. You'll need pieces of coal or stones for eyes and buttons, a carrot for his nose, and so on.

**The challenge is to make the biggest snow-man in the whole world.**

# A NEWSY LETTER

In our alphabet, as you know, we have 26 letters—
A B C D E F G H I J K L M N O P Q R S T U V W X
Y Z—but in some countries they have fewer
letters, and in others many more. Do you think we
use all of them all of the time? Or are there some
that we use so little that we could really do without
them?

Take a sheet from a newspaper, or a page
from a magazine that has a lot of writing
on it and very few pictures. Now look for
each letter of the alphabet in turn. First
look for the letter A and when you have
found one put a circle around it, look for
a letter B, and so on until you reach the
letter Z.

If you get to the stage where you want a
particular letter and it does not appear
on the page, you will have to find
**another page** and start from A again.

**The challenge is to find a page that contains
every single letter of the alphabet.** Is there one
particular letter that does not appear on any page? If
so, perhaps it is the one we could do without...

# PENNY
# BALANCING

This challenge will not only
amaze your friends, it will
amaze you too! You have got
to balance a penny on the
end of a coat hanger and
swing the hanger around
in a circle without the
penny falling off.

Take a wire coat hanger that has a flat
end and bend it as shown in the picture:

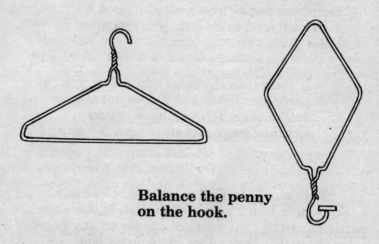

**Balance the penny
on the hook.**

With a little practice you will be able to
swing the hanger round in a circle and,
believe it or not, the penny won't fall off!

# LIGHT SPONGE

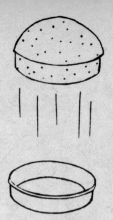

**The challenge is to make the lightest and most delicious sponge cake in the world.**

**You will need:—**

> **2 eggs**
> **75g (3oz) caster sugar**
> **75g (3oz) self raising flour**

Heat the oven to 180°C, 350°F or gas mark 4, and lightly grease an 18cm (7 ins) cake tin.

Break the eggs into a bowl, and whisk them very lightly, then add the sugar.

Now beat them very very quickly with a fork or whisk until the mixture becomes almost white and really creamy. The secret of a good sponge is in the beating.

When you have done this, fold in the flour, a spoonful at a time. Pour the mixture immediately into the prepared cake tin and place it in the centre of the pre-heated oven for 30 minutes. Always use oven gloves to take things in and out of an oven—or ask an adult to do it for you.

If you have beaten the mixture really well it will rise into a beautifully light and fluffy sponge. Turn the sponge out onto a wire rack to cool. When cold, split the cake and fill it with jam and cream, or lemon curd, or any filling you wish. This is a challenge you can eat!

# SKIP IT

Skipping can be tremendous fun and a real challenge too.

If you have a really long rope, get a friend to take one end and another friend to take the other end and get them to swing the rope and see if you can skip **100 times without stopping**. Take it in turns to see who can skip the longest.

If you have several friends, then a real challenge is to take a long rope, with one person at each end to swing it, and two, three, or four of you can stand in a row and all skip at the same time over the same rope. Each time one of you touches the rope he or she must drop out, until eventually only one person is left. That one is the champion.

If you only have smaller skipping ropes
you can all skip individually, the
champion being the one who can
continue skipping the longest without
stopping.

In 1980, Katsumi Suzuki of Japan
skipped non-stop for 9 hours and 46
minutes. The most people who have ever
skipped on one rope **at the same time** is
65!

# STATUES

I'm sure you have seen statues and shop window
dummies, and other figures that look like real people
but stand perfectly still without moving. Have you
ever wondered what it is like to be a statue, how
difficult it must be not being able to move whatever
happens? If the Statue of Liberty gets cramp in her
arm she cannot rub it, not until everybody is asleep
anyway. Imagine what it is like for Nelson on the
top of his column; however much the pigeons tickle
him he cannot shoo them away, laugh or scratch
himself. It's tough being a statue.

**As a challenge, see if you can turn
yourself into a statue for five minutes.**

Stand up straight, and put your arms in a comfortable position. Once you have adopted the pose of a statue, imagine that you are Nelson on his column for five minutes and whatever happens you cannot and must not move. Even if World War III breaks out during those five minutes, or the house falls down, or your favourite television programme begins, **you must not move a muscle**.

If you succeed you may be well on your way to taking over from Nelson when he goes on holiday next, but whatever you do, don't stand still for longer than five minutes. Who knows, if the wind changed you might turn to stone—and turning you back again is a challenge that even this book couldn't help you with.

# HAND SIGNALS

If you have ever stood in a crowded room and wanted to communicate with a friend on the other side you may have told him or her what you wanted by using sign language. You may have pointed to your mouth if you were hungry, or put your hand in the shape of a cup if you were thirsty, or held your hand to your ear meaning that he or she was wanted on the telephone, or even tapped yourself gently on the head to imply that you thought someone or something was quite mad! People who are deaf use a proper sign language in which they have a different hand shape for each letter of the alphabet so that they can spell out whole words, and have certain signs to express whole words. If you have ever turned the sound down on the television and simply watched people's actions you will be surprised how often people move their hands when they are explaining something or expressing something, and it is often possible to understand exactly what is happening without hearing a single word.

**As a challenge, set aside some time with your friends when not one of you is going to speak.** Instead you are going to communicate using only your hands.

Imagine that you are in a foreign country and cannot speak the language and need to make yourself understood. You will find it very challenging.

# HAPPY PEOPLE

This challenge will not only take great courage, but will also prove to you how many happy people there are around. As you travel along in a car, pick out a person on the side of the road, give them a big smile and wave to them as you drive past. **The challenge is to do it so nicely that they smile and wave back.**

If you have a grin rather than a smile they will think that you are laughing at them and will feel offended, so practise your pleasant smiles very carefully. If the whole family waves at one particular person as you go by they will probably wave at you thinking that they must know you, and they will spend the whole day puzzling over who you were!

If you are successful in this challenge, everybody you wave to will wave back, and you will have proved the truth of the old saying: 'The smile you give to the world comes back to you'.

# LOOPY CHALLENGE

Take a length of string, approximately one metre long, and make a loop out of it by tying the two ends together in a knot.

Stand with your legs apart, place the loop over your right arm and put your right hand in your pocket. Now try and remove the loop from your body **without taking your right hand out of your pocket**.

**CLUE:**
*Make sure your coat is off
Your right hand pocketed
While o'er your arm
An endless string
A metre round.*

*Take the string off
But for fun,
It must be done
Keeping your right hand in place
And no smile on your face.*

*Until you sort this challenge out
No coat shall wrap your back about.*

(If you want a further hint of how to do it look on page 156.)

# HOW FAST?

Many animals can run faster than man. If you've
been in a park with a dog you will know that he or
she can shoot off much faster than you can! The
fastest speed that a man has ever reached is 43
km per hour which was achieved by Robert Lee
Hayes of Florida, USA, when he was twenty-one.
The fastest animal is the cheetah which can reach
speeds of up to 101 km per hour.

You may not be a record breaker yet, but
what is the fastest time in which you can
run 100 metres, 200 metres, 500 metres
and 1000 metres?

Make yourself a chart so that you can
check your records:

| NAME | DISTANCE | TIME | DATE |
|------|----------|------|------|

CHEETAH

114

# BACK TO FRONT

For this challenge you will need **a mirror** you can sit in front of, and a **piece of paper** and **a pencil**.

**Looking only in the mirror,** and not at your hand, write your name so it appears the right way round in the mirror. When you have completed this, look at your piece of paper—how does your name appear now?

Again, looking into the mirror, draw a face making sure that the eyes, nose and mouth are in the correct place.

Finally, draw a square, remembering always to look only in the mirror and never at your piece of paper.

CHEATER

# BLIND AS A
# BAT

For this challenge you will need some **paper cups, children's building blocks**, and **pencil and paper**.

First of all, get someone to blindfold you with a scarf, making sure that you cannot see anything at all. There's to be no cheating by peeping!

1. When blindfolded take the pencil in your hand and draw four squares, one at a time. Try to draw them one above the other as if they were in a pile.

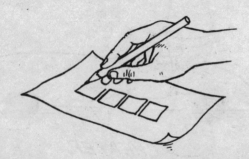

**2.** Still blindfolded, take the building blocks one at a time and attempt to build them into a tower as your picture should have been.

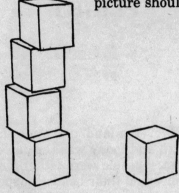

**3.** Finally, take some paper cups and build them into a tower with rims and bases touching, like this:—

# THE PRISONER'S PLIGHT

In a prison in a far-off foreign land, a prisoner had been sentenced to death and today was the day of his execution. In this country people were either put to death by hanging or else had their heads chopped off.

This prisoner, however, was given one last chance to save his life. He was told that he could save himself with one simple statement—but there was a catch.

The jailer said:

> *'If you tell the truth you will have your head cut off; if you lie you will be hanged.'*

The prisoner thought for a short time and made his statement. Fortunately he said exactly the right thing and his life was spared.

Imagine that you are that prisoner and you are faced with such a challenge, what would you say?

118                           **Solution on page 157.**

# PENNY PILE

For this challenge you will need **4 pennies,** or you can use four 5p pieces if you've just won the Pools or the Premium Bonds.

Place one coin on the tip of each of your fingers, covering the nail:—

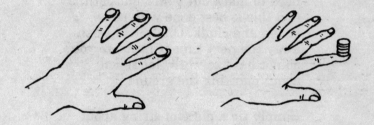

Without using your thumb, or your left hand in any way, work all the four coins into a pile on your first finger. It can be done!

If at any time the coins fall off, even if you have got three in a pile and just one more to go, you must start again from the beginning. No cheating!

# BICYCLE MARATHON

If you and some friends have bicycles you can have
your very own bicycle marathon. You'll need
somewhere where there is no traffic: your local park
might have an area where you can cycle, or you may
have a large garden where you can ride in safety.

**Here are your bicycle challenges:**

I. **Double-quick-Speed** For this you
   need to mark out a straight path
   and this is best done with some
   string and chalk. Chalk will wash
   away the next time it rains, so you
   do not have to worry too much
   about marking the ground.

   Simply tie a piece of string about
   1 metre long to two pieces of chalk
   so that there is a piece on each
   end.

I METRE OF STRING

CHALK

If you take one piece of chalk and
a friend takes the other, you
can pull the string tight and
make two straight lines the
full length of your course.

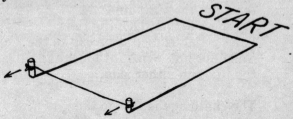

A tape-measure would be useful to
mark out the length of the course,
although this is not essential as
long as all riders are doing the
same course.

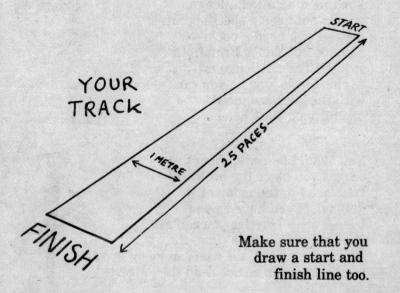

YOUR
TRACK

Make sure that you
draw a start and
finish line too.

For the challenge you
will need a stop watch
to time each rider. One
at a time the riders begin
with their front wheel just
touching the start line
When you shout GO! the rider
must pedal as fast as he can to the
finishing line, **without** touching
the lines on either side.

The challenge is to ride the
course in the fastest possible time.

## II. Posture Pedalling

For this difficult challenge
you do not need a specific course;
instead you need a book—
any book by Gyles Brandreth
will do. The challenge is
to ride for as long as you can
with the book balanced
carefully on your head.

You should be timed from the
second you place the book on
your head to the moment it
falls off. If you have several
friends with bicycles you can all
start off at the same time, the
winner being the one who can keep
the book on his or her head the longest.

### III. Spiral Cycle With this challenge you need to mark out the course with chalk like this:

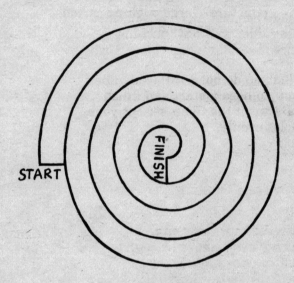

The challenge is to ride through the course without touching the lines. Each rider should be timed separately.

IV. **Obstacle Course** For the Obstacle Course challenge you will need some obstacles. There are many things you can use, such as small cardboard boxes, plastic orange squash bottles (do not use glass in case they break and you get a puncture), large yoghurt cartons, skittles, and so on.

For this you do not need a side line, but you do need a start and finish line. Between the lines, set out your obstacles evenly.

The challenge is to ride the course on your bicycle, weaving carefully in between each obstacle without touching any of them. If you do you are disqualified.

**V. Double-Slow-Time** This challenge is similar to challenge I except that the object is to do the course in the **slowest** possible time. You start with your front wheel on the starting line as before and after the shout GO! you move off as slowly as you can. This will be a great test of balance and steering abilities for if you wobble at all you will touch the side-line and be disqualified.

# HAND IT TO YOURSELF

For this challenge you will need some **plaster of Paris** and **an old rubber glove**, perhaps an odd one that is left from an old pair—but make sure it has no holes in it.

**Your challenge is to make a hand!** It's not as impossible as it sounds. All you need is some quick-setting plaster which you mix with water; this can be bought quite cheaply at any model shop.

Once you have mixed it into a fairly runny mixture pour it into the rubber glove.

Hang it with a couple of pegs to set.

Plaster of Paris
takes about 20–30
minutes to set.

When the plaster is perfectly hard you can carefully
peel off the glove and you should have a hand. You
can paint it any colour you wish. Make a pair and
use them as book-ends. The same glove can be used
over and over again if you are careful. If you move
the fingers of the glove before the plaster sets, you
can bend the fingers of your hand into different
positions.

You'll just have to hand it to yourself: it's a creative
challenge that will amaze your friends when they
see your beautifully sculptured hands!

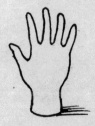

# MASTER DETECTIVE

You too can be a Master Detective like Sherlock Holmes or Sexton Blake. **All you have to do is take the fingerprints of your friends and members of your family.**

Simply take one of their fingers and roll it on an ink pad, then press it down firmly onto a piece of white paper, taking great care not to smudge the print as you do so. Make sure that you label each print so that you know exactly whose it is for future reference.

MUM

DAD

SUSAN

**PETER**

**GRANDAD**

**The challenge is to take a particular object in your house, for example, a door handle or milkbottle, and find out from the prints exactly who has touched it.**

You can do this by dusting the object very carefully with a small paintbrush and a little talcum powder. Having done your delicate dusting you need to press a piece of sellotape onto the prints and 'lift' them off. If you put the piece of sellotape onto a piece of black card you will then have the fingerprint permanently. If you have taken the fingerprints of all the members of your household you will be able to match up the circles and wavy lines of the print and find out exactly who has touched it.

It is a surprising fact, but no two people in the world have the same fingerprint which is why the police take fingerprints to help them catch criminals. People can disguise their faces and features, but nothing will change the fingerprints you are born with.

# BRAINBUSTERS: 5

Here are the most difficult
mental challenges of
them all!

**a.** A man has to cross a river by boat,
but there is a rule that says he may
only take **one object** across with him
at a time. He has a cabbage, a goat
and a fox. This means that on each
trip he has to leave two things on one
side of the river. He cannot leave the
goat with the cabbage because the
goat would eat it. Neither can he
leave the fox and the goat together
because the fox would kill the goat,
How can he take all the things safely
across to the opposite side of the river?

**b.** *What we caught we threw away.*
*What we could not catch we kept.*

What is it?

**c.** In this rhyme three words are
missing. Each of the missing words
contain exactly the same letters.
What are the missing words?

> *Through the ****** trees*
> *Softly coo the doves;*
> *Let a ****** breeze*
> ******* youthful loves.*

**d.** If six cats can catch six mice in 1/10 of
an hour, how many cats would it take
to catch 100 mice in 6,000 seconds?

**e.** A farmer's wife sold to Mr. Brown
half her supply of eggs and half an
egg. She then sold to Mr. White half
of her remaining stock and half an
egg. Then Mr. Green bought half of
the eggs which she had left and half
an egg. Finally Miss Pink bought the
rest of the stock which was 33 eggs.
How many eggs did she have to start
with? She did not have any broken
eggs.

**Solutions on page 157.**

# WHERE HAVE YOU BEAN?

For this challenge you don't need to be clever; you don't need green fingers; you don't even need magic words. You simply need **2 runner bean seeds; two jam jars; some blotting paper; and some water.**

Into each jam jar put a tube of blotting paper so that it touches the side of the jar all the way round.

If you damp the blotting paper first you will find that it will stick to the sides.

Into each jar push one
bean so that it is between
the blotting paper and
the jar.

Finally put about five
centimetres of water into
the bottom of the jar.

In a matter of days the beans will begin
to grow and you will see them grow a
little bit more each day. But this is the
challenge:—

**DO THE BEANS GROW FASTER IN
THE DARK OR IN THE LIGHT?**

Keep one jar in a dark cupboard with no
chinks of light, and stand the other jar
on a window sill so that it is in the light.
Now all you need is patience to wait and
watch!

# HOW STRONG?

Challenge a friend to tell you how strong he thinks an ordinary piece of paper is: ask him how many books he thinks the piece of paper could support before it collapsed.

To test his guess, take an ordinary sheet of paper and roll it into a tube, fixing it with some sellotape.

Stand the tube on the table like this:

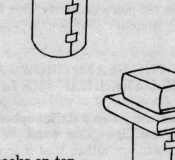

And pile the books on top, one at a time.

See if your friend was right. Did the paper hold the number of books he said it would? Did it hold more? Did it hold fewer?

# BLOATED BALLOONS

For this challenge you will need:—

1. **Some balloons**
2. **Some water**
3. **Some old waterproof clothes**
4. **A very good friend!**

This challenge can be very messy so **always** do it outside, and wear as much waterproof clothing as possible, just in case you are not as careful as you mean to be and things go wrong!

When dressed in your waterproof clothes, fill a balloon with some water: between 250–500 ml (½–1 pint), depending on how big your balloon is, but do not fill it too full or it will burst and you **will** get wet. Then very carefully tie a knot in the end, again taking great care or the water will squirt at you like a hose-pipe.

You now have a nice squelchy ball. You will find it is really quite tough, so long as you do not drop it on the ground or prick it in any way. The idea is to throw it carefully to each other and **catch** it. You must keep it in the air all the time because if you drop it it'll burst and you might get wet. The challenge is to keep the balloon whole, and not get wet!

135

# PROVERBS

A proverb is a maxim or little rhyme that usually contains some words of wisdom well worth remembering. For example, you may have heard one of your older (and wiser) relations uttering 'The devil finds work for idle hands', which is a proverbial way of saying that you should always keep busy to keep out of trouble because someone with nothing to do is likely to get into mischief. Here are some well-known proverbs in the form of a rhyme, but some words have been missed out. Can you fill in the blanks?

Fast bind and fast find, have two
strings to your ____;
Contentment is better than ____you
know.

The devil finds work for hands ____to
do,
A miss is as good as a ____is to you.

136

You speak of the ____ he's sure to
appear;
You can't make a silk purse out of
a _____ _____

A man by his ____ always is known;
Who lives in a glass house should not
throw a ____.

When the blind leads the ____ both
will fall in the ditch;
It's better born lucky than being born
____.

Little pitchers have big ____; burnt
child dreads the ____;
Though speaking the ____, no one
credits a liar.

Speech may be ____, but silence
is ____;
There's never a ____ like the ____ who
is old.

Answers on page 157.

# SIGN FOR IT

If you enjoy watching television, or going to concerts, or listening to the radio, or if you happen to have a favourite football team, this is a challenge which you should find particularly enjoyable.

> **Choose a group of entertainers—
> actors or cricketers or racing drivers
> or pop stars—and collect as many
> autographs as you can.**

If you go to the theatre you will find that every theatre has a stage door, usually at the back or side of the building, and this is where the stars appearing at the theatre will come in and out. If you wait outside the stage door of a theatre where your favourite actor is appearing, sooner or later he will come along and if you ask him very nicely he will give you his autograph. Make sure you have a note pad, or proper autograph book, and a pen with you at all times.

If you have a favourite football team then set out to collect the autographs of **every** member of that team. Or if you have a favourite television programme see how many of the actors' autographs from that programme you can get.

Don't worry if you do not live close to a theatre; you can always write to your favourite TV stars, telling them your name and address, how old you are, and that you would like to have their autograph in your collection. Do remember to enclose a stamped and addressed envelope with your letter so that they can send their signature back to you. If you are very lucky you might even get some autographed photographs sent to you too. Don't, however, write to Buckingham Palace and ask for the Queen's autograph, or for those of the Prince and Princess of Wales, because they are not allowed to give them.

The word 'autograph' actually comes from the Greek and means 'self-writing'. Most people take the word 'autograph' to mean 'signature', but in fact an autograph can be absolutely anything from a single word to a whole page of handwriting. Some people make a hobby of collecting very rare and sought-after autographs—for example, the signatures of Napoleon or Marie Curie or the Duke of Wellington or Nelson, or a famous inventor or explorer. Such autographs are worth a great deal of money, especially if the person happened to live for only a short time so that there are very few of their signatures in existence. It is fun to collect all sorts of autographs, but some people like to specialise and collect only signatures of Prime Ministers, or only signatures of scientists, which is much more of a challenge. As your own autograph collection grows you may be interested to see the autographs of famous figures from history. These can often be seen on very old manuscripts in museums, or, from your local library, you can borrow 'The Guinness Book of World Autographs' which features copies of hundreds of exciting autographs.

Here is a copy of my signature:

I challenge you to get an original version of it for your autograph collection.

# BACK TO FRONT

You may be incredibly quick
at dressing yourself in
the mornings (and if you ever
go on the stage you will
find that the art of doing a
'quick change' is very
important), but, whether
you are quick or slow
at dressing, as a challenge
**see if you can put your
coat on back to front so
that the buttons are at
the back.**

Without any assistance, attempt to do up
all the buttons, starting from the bottom
and working your way to the top.

Having performed this task, if you now walk
backwards people will think that you have twisted
your head back to front! (I once knew a girl who was
a keen cyclist and she always wore her coat back to
front to protect herself from the wind. Unfortunately
one day she fell off her bicycle in the middle of the
market square and at the foot of a policeman. Her
mother happened to be out shopping and seeing her
daughter, she dashed over to the policeman to see if
the girl was all right.

'Oh yes, she's fine,' said the policeman, 'now that
I've turned her head the right way round!')

# IT'S A MATCH

**a.** Take **sixteen matchsticks** or cocktail sticks and lay them down to form ten triangles:

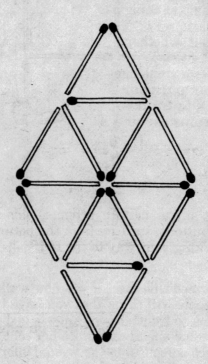

Take away just **four** matches and leave four triangles only.

**b.** Lay the matches down to form five squares. Move **three** matches to form four squares of equal size

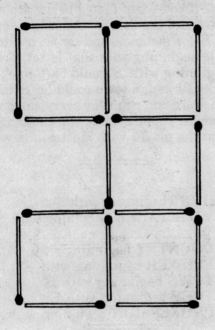

**Solution on page 158.**

# IT BEGINS WITH...

This is a challenge that you can tackle on your own or with friends. You can even turn it into a quiet party game if you wish. Listed below are a number of categories and the idea is to choose a letter of the alphabet, 'S' for instance, and for each category find an example beginning with that letter. For example, a river beginning with 'S' could be 'Seine', a flower could be 'Sunflower', a town could be 'Salisbury' and so on. You score one point for every category you complete and if you are doing the challenge as a competition the player with most points wins.

Name a **RIVER** beginning with 'S' ..............................
Name a **VEGETABLE** beginning with 'S' ..................................................................
Name a **COUNTRY** beginning with 'S' ...
Name a **FLOWER** beginning with 'S' .....
Name a **TOWN** beginning with 'S' ...........
Name a **TREE** beginning with 'S' ............
Name a **PROFESSION** beginning with 'S' ..................................................................
Give a **BOY's NAME** beginning with 'S'
Give a **GIRL's NAME** beginning with 'S'
Name an **ARTICLE OF CLOTHING** beginning with 'S' .......................................
Name an **ANIMAL** beginning with 'S' ....
Name a **TELEVISION CHARACTER** beginning with 'S' .......................................

# PASS THE GLASS

Borrow **two wine glasses** that have round, bowl-shaped, bottoms:—

Place a two-pence piece in one of the glasses. If you blow very hard onto the coin it will spin round and hop out of one glass into the other!

Having successfully risen to the first challenge, put a one-pence piece and a two-pence piece into a glass like this:—

Now if you blow very hard onto the two-pence piece it will spin round and the one-pence piece will be blown out on to the table!

145

# HURDLES

The fastest time recorded for running the 110 metre hurdles is 13 seconds. You may not be an Olympic record breaker, but you can set your own hurdle record.

First of all you will need to set out your course. Use a strip of your garden or a nearby park or playground. If your garden is only ten metres long you will simply have to run backwards and forwards ten times until you have completed 100 metres.

For your hurdles you need obstacles that are neither hard nor sharp as you do not want to hurt yourself if you accidentally run into them. Cardboard boxes are ideal: you can stand them at equal distances and use them to jump over. Alternatively you can take equal sized sticks and tie some string to them. Push the sticks lightly into the ground so that if you do happen to catch your foot on them they will lift straight out of the ground and you won't trip.

Having set out your course, start running and jumping. Get someone to time you with a stopwatch. Persuade your friends to run the same course and discover who is the fastest hurdler of them all.

# BEACH CHALLENGE

Next time you are on a beach, this is what you've got to do:

1. Build the tallest sand castle that you can.

2. Dig a hole as deep as you can.

**3.** Build a sand castle on the water's edge as the tide is coming in, and make it so firm that as the sea splashes around it the castle does not crumble.

**4.** Dig a deep hole at least 5 metres from the sea. When you have dug it, collect sea water from the sea and try and fill the hole completely with water.

**5.** Build a sand castle and cover it **completely** with small pebbles and shells so that no sand is showing.

**6.** The next time your father or mother or another grown-up goes to sleep in their deck chair, carefully try to bury their feet in the sand **without them knowing it**.

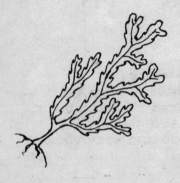

# SOLUTIONS

## SOLUTIONS TO BRAINBUSTERS: 1

**a.**

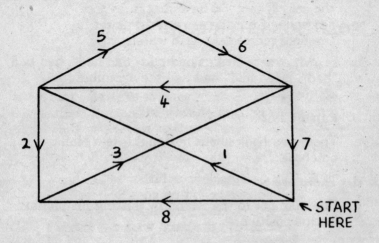

**b.** Emma was flying in a plane from Los Angeles to Tokyo and crossed the date line just at midnight so the date changed from June 8th to June 10th. Emma's birthday is June 9th.

**c.** 20 years ago.

**d.** Daughter.

**e.** Feathers, because they are weighed by avoirdupois weight and gold by Troy weight! If, however, you weighed a pound of feathers and a pound of gold on the same scale then neither would be heavier; they would both be the same weight.

## THE MAN FROM ST. IVES

If you were very clever you would have noticed that only the 'I' of the rhyme is going to St. Ives, so the answer to the question is actually 1! The man, his wives, their cats and kits add up to 400 in all, but they were coming **from** St. Ives.

## SOLUTIONS TO BRAINBUSTERS: 2

**a.** Brown, where Briggs had had "had had", had had "had". "Had had" had had the examiners' approval.

**b.** Pamela is 24.

**c.** There is a book about nothing: it is a blank notebook.

**d.** There are six cats.

**e.** The man got to the island by putting his planks in this position:—

# SHAPE THE FLOOR

## CROSS COINS

Lift the top and bottom coin of the vertical arm and pile them on the centre coin. The cross will then count five in both directions!

## SOLUTIONS TO BRAINBUSTERS: 3

1. Sunday

2. The man would be 99 years old. There was no year 0: we went straight from year 1 BC to year 1 AD.

3. He is her son, so the relationship is 'Mother'.

4. Only two hours. Setting the clock at 8 PM it would go off at 10 PM, being only a twelve hour clock.

**5.** You can put the number 10,000 in a circle if you fold your paper—

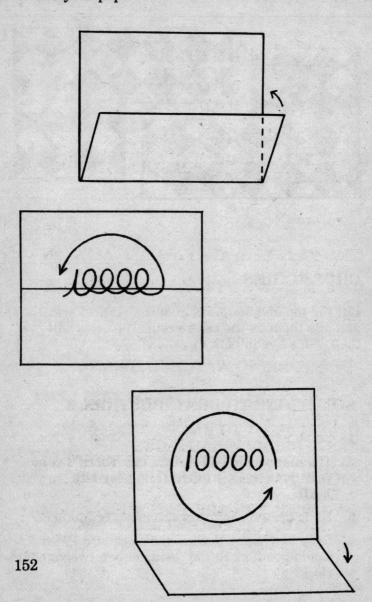

## MUMS AND DADS

The moves are like this—

| | |
|---|---|
| Start | D M D M D M |
| Move 1 | D M D M M D |
| Move 2 | D D M M M D |
| Move 3 | D D D M M M |

## FISHY CHALLENGE

Fisherman 3.

## CRACK THE CODE

1. THE RAIN IN SPAIN FALLS MAINLY ON THE PLAIN.
2. THIS IS QUITE A CHALLENGE BUT NOT DIFFICULT FOR SOMEONE WHO IS REALLY CLEVER.
3. MEET ME TONIGHT AT THE OLD CHURCH AT MIDNIGHT.
4. WE ARE BEING WATCHED BY AN ENEMY AGENT.
5. CAN YOU CRACK THIS CODE IT IS VERY DIFFICULT.
6. IF YOU WANT TO KNOW THE SECRET PASSWORD IT IS SAUSAGES.
7. I THINK ROBERT IS A COUNTER SPY AND IS WORKING FOR THE ENEMY AGENT.
8. TWO WISE YOU ARE TWO WISE YOU BE I SEE YOU ARE TWO WISE FOR ME.

## JOIN THE DOTS

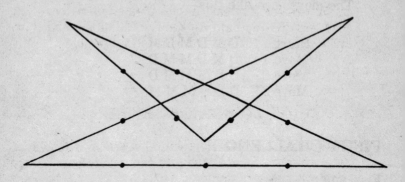

## HOW FAR?

The air hostess will travel the farthest—by walking up and down throughout the journey!

## A CUT ABOVE

This is how it should be done:—

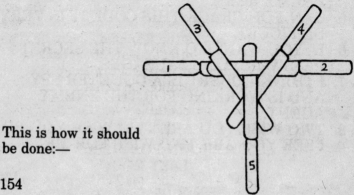

Lay the four knives down in the same order as the numbers on the handles. To lift them you simply pass the fifth knife **over** numbers 3 and 4, and **under** knives 1 and 2. You should then find that just by holding the handle of the fifth knife you can lift all five knives in one go.

## SOLUTIONS TO BRAINBUSTERS: 4

**a.** When the man is a clergyman, a priest, a Rabbi or a Justice of the Peace and can actually perform the ceremony.

**b.** Peter.

**c.** You can work this out yourself very easily by using different coloured counters for the missionaries and the cannibals. You will find that seven trips are needed.

**d.** Mr. Wood is 69 years and 12 weeks old.
Miss Wood is 30 years and 40 weeks old.

**e.** A heptagon.

**f.** The painting looks wrong because what the artist is actually painting is a mirror image of himself because this is what he thinks he looks like, but in a mirror everything appears to be back to front. If the portrait were held in front of a mirror it would look like the artist.

**g.** One sentence that contains every letter of the alphabet is:

THE QUICK BROWN FOX JUMPS OVER THE
LAZY DOG.

You saw it first on page 70.

## HOW MANY

There are 14 triangles in all.

## TRICKY TRIANGLE

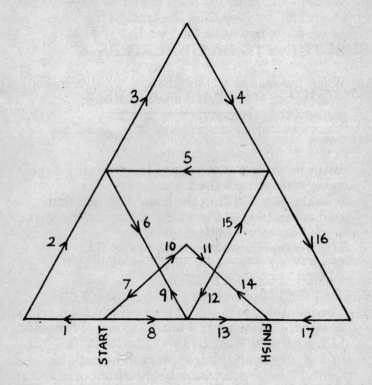

## LOOPY CHALLENGE

The clue is not to wear a coat, but a sleeveless
sweater or waistcoat. If you pass the string
through the sleeve and over your head, you will
find the challenge can be done.

# THE PRISONER'S PLIGHT

The statement that saved his life was: "I will be hanged." He cannot be hanged because that would mean that he was telling the truth and he can only be hanged for telling a lie. He cannot, however, have his head cut off because then he would not be telling the truth if this happened, so he had to be set free. Did you get it right?

# SOLUTIONS TO BRAINBUSTERS: 5

**a.** These are the crossings that the man made:—
1. He crossed with the goat.
2. He returned emptyhanded.
3. He crossed with the fox.
4. He returned taking the goat back with him.
5. He crossed with the cabbage, leaving the goat.
6. He came back emptyhanded.
7. He crossed with the goat.

**b.** Fleas.
**c.** FOREST; SOFTER; FOSTER.
**d.** 6 cats eat 100 mice in the 100 minutes (6,000 seconds)
**e.** 271 eggs.

# PROVERBS

Fast bind and fast find, have two strings to your
   **bow**;
Contentment is better than **sorrow** you know.

The devil finds work for hands **idle** to do;
A miss is as good as a **mile** is to you.

You speak of the **devil** he's sure to appear;
You can't make a silk purse from out a **sow's ear**.

A man by his **face** always is known;
Who lives in a glass house should not throw a **stone**.

When the blind leads the **blind** both will fall in the ditch;
It's better born lucky than being born **rich**.

Little pitchers have big **mouths**; burnt child dreads the **fire**;
Though speaking the **truth**, no-one credits a liar.

Speech may be **silver**, but silence is **gold**;
There's never a **fool** like the **fool** who is old.

## IT'S A MATCH

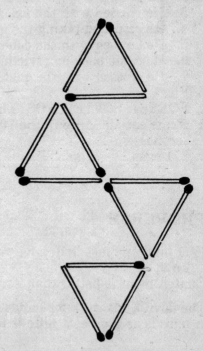

a.

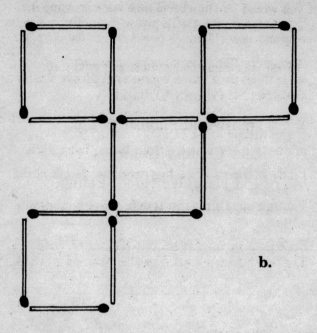

b.

If you would like to receive a newsletter telling you about our new children's books, fill in the coupon with your name and address and send it to:

**Gillian Osband,**

**Transworld Publishers Ltd,**

**Century House,**

**61–63 Uxbridge Road, Ealing,**

**London, W5 5SA**

Name .........................................................................

Address .....................................................................

.................................................................................

## CHILDREN'S NEWSLETTER

All the books on the previous pages are available at your bookshop or can be ordered direct from Transworld Publishers Ltd., Cash Sales Dept. P.O. Box 11, Falmouth, Cornwall.

Please send full name and address together with cheque or postal order—no currency, and allow 40p per book to cover postage and packing (plus 18p each for additional copies).